BEDROOM VOWEL

BUNNY, an imprint of Fonograf Editions
Edited by Adie B. Steckel, Ellena Basada & Jeff Alessandrelli
Portland, OR & New York City, NY

Copyright © 2023 by Zoe Tuck • All rights reserved
Cover art by Audra Puchalski
Cover and text design by Mike Corrao

First Edition, Second Printing

BUNNY03

Published by BUNNY c/o Fonograf Editions
www.bunnypresse.org
www.fonografeditions.com

For information about permission to reuse any material from this book,
please contact BUNNY at bunnypresse@gmail.com.

Distributed by NYU Press
NYUPress.org

The manufacturer's authorized representative in the EU for product safety
is Mare Nostrum Group B.V., Mauritskade 21D, 1091 GC Amsterdam,
The Netherlands. Email: gpsr@mare-nostrum.co.uk.

[clmp]

Fonograf Editions is a proud member of the Community of Literary
Magazines and Presses

ISBN: 978-1-7378036-9-0
ISBN (ebook): 978-1-964499-20-8
LCCN: 2023930329

BEDROOM VOWEL

Zoe Tuck

BUNNY

for Britt

CONTENTS

Time Travel / 11

Early Edition / 13

Art Criticism / 15

Coneys in Vilnius / 16

Samson's Riddle / 17

Ordinary Water / 19

PowerXtreme / 21

What's happening in the troposphere / 23

Every morning / 25

A little estuary / 27

My opposites / 29

No sunlight / 31

Daily Poem / 33

In the bath I didn't take / 34

Epistolary / 36

Exit / 39

Poem for Hoa / 40

Smol Bean / 43

Dear Diary / 46

Mouthful / 48

Chassis / 50

A boring poem / 51

Janáček's Enigmatic Tones / 54

Dear LL and VS / 58

Thanatopsis / 63

Thanatopsis Written Using Generative Techniques of
Karinne Keithley Syers / 64

A little pile / 66

Your valid extended play remix / 69

The Fence / 72

Well-known eccentrics / 75

The Painting of My Life / 77

La la la / 79

Alternative Poetry / 81

Being alive / 84

Dragging My Feet / 85

A Poem About Simone Weil / 87

A Little Sparrow / 89

Stargate Star Friend / 92

Field research / 93

Early Hominids / 95

Awaiter / 97

Barking / 99

500,000 people dead of COVID in the US & I'm sorry
that being on my HD tip is how I process it / 101

I'm not as bad as I pretended to be / 103

The Women's Building / 105

Ars Poetica / 109

Autonomous Zones / 111

Comet / 113

One time, years ago now, Alana sent me a recording of
late-stage Elvis performing in Vegas because it made
her think of me / 115

El Tiempo / 117

Midnight Movie / 118

Hymns to the Night / 119

One, two, three, four / 121

Pavilion / 123

Ghazal With Ill-Chosen Repeating Word / 124

Notes / 127

Time Travel

I woke up

Britt and Patsy were there

coffee, even without cream

and I ate the rest of the chèvre

on the salty little rice crackers

that Patsy and I both love

I didn't have any work due today

I read Leora's piece and I really liked it

I had the idea to write poems for people

if they donate to Trans Asylum Seeker Support Network

which gives me an excuse to spend time

writing one-off poems

each one of which can exist within its own universe of rules

their only common denominator being my reasons

and my sentiments.

My therapist had me externalize "sad me" from the other day and
talk to her

It was a little bit like time travel

I imagined that I was literally sitting across from her

glum with her elbows on her knees and her fists propping up her
cheeks

and in this way, it was easier to sympathize with her as I would a
friend.

It was a ritual and I liked that.

My friend Zach called during therapy.

I called him back after and we talked for an hour
about going to the Madonna Inn or renting a block of rooms
with a group of friends in a gay resort in the Poconos
to celebrate the end of the pandemic someday.
For a second, I imagined having a regular-ass vulva
(but I wasn't sad about it)
and cum like okra, nopales, a broken stalk of aloe vera
I ordered delicious sandwiches for Britt and I
from a bakery in Easthampton
and drove there with the window down
listening to Green Day
slapping my hand against the car
and thinking about band practice on Sunday
It's good to have something to look forward to, like:
I might walk around later with Emily
I might go for a run
I'll probably carve out some time to write
a letter to Pop, my oldest living family member,
who I never came out, and so he is also the last person
to call me the name I was given at birth

Early Edition

for Paula Mendoza

A week ago, as if on a tv show
in which a haunting manifests through water,
I opened my mouth to scream,
and it just came spilling out—
and yet I didn't drown,
like the mouse dropped into
the vat of oxygenated liquid
that I read about in a *Weekly Reader*
at some point in the 90s.
They (the mouse) thought they were drowning
and panicked but then breathed in
and discovered it was possible
even though it contradicted
their brain-stem-deep knowledge.

Mouse-related news items from childhood
really stay with me. Yes, we all talked
when they cloned the sheep but
more chilling for my childhood brain
was how and more importantly why
did they grow a human ear on the back of a mouse?
We weren't kids together but we were kids
at around the same time—did you get *Weekly Reade*r in Surrey?
Today I get the news from whatever

poets share on social media (god help me),
Democracy Now, until they started talking
about the DNC today and I just couldn't,
and *The Shoestring* for local stuff,
Jonathan Myerson Katz's *The Long Version*,
which I forget how I found my way to,
but which really is meaty and internationalist
in its perspective,
and memes,
and masked mouths,
and unmasked mouths at a greater distance,
and around the edges of writing on art and culture.
If we reach Paradise
(which I pursue playfully, exegetically, foolishly)
how will it be reported?

Art Criticism

for Kalmia Strong

Galleries or the bijoux (or is that billet-doux)

pirouetting through the pages

it might be an axiom of applied utopianism (life) that something
goes wrong

Sometimes I mean to write "criticism," but it comes out as a poem.

silly and baroque, his Dionysian masculinity

I was young and I thought that all art would be like this: lush and
arcane

tonnes of ooze, costumery, Detroit autos, the perfect ashlar,

aeolian harps resounding in the elevator shaft.

The shoes she used to cut the potatoes were sex to me—I can't
explain it!

the night wore on and we marched down the warm street in ludic
cacophony;

being desiring to know itself and thus becoming more than one

through narrative and staging into psychogeographic engagement
with the city.

Coneys in Vilnius

for Brianna, TASSN donor

Podría escribir un poema en español
(aunque nunca lo he hecho), pero
cuando empecé a escribir en inglés,
el poema—que debía ser sobre Vilnius—sufrió
un cortocircuitó porque me caí
en una madriguera de conejo
sobre la trágica historia de la ciudad en el siglo XX.
Así que, en lugar de escribir un poema sobre Vilnius en inglés,
te escribo un poema sobre mi fracaso
en escribir sobre Vilnius en inglés, en español.
En la brecha entre los dos idiomas,
donde van las cosas indecibles.

Samson's Riddle

for Kimberly Alidio

I tried to write you the last poem of the night
but I was all tuckered out, so you get
the first poem of the morning, which
for mystical reasons, contains an element
of the abandoned poem:
sliced raw red onion on pumpernickel
which now, by virtue of its removal from context
takes on an air of mystery
Do you like when the recondite flowers in the mundane?
This germination daily reignites the fires of the Kitchen of the World—
that is, the holy place where existence recapitulates itself
out of pure generosity. Therefore, every ordinary kitchen
like yours or mine, is a face of a geometrical phantasy
with innumerably many sides. What an honor!
Sliced raw red onion on pumpernickel:
it sounds healthy I guess but not especially flavorful
but its aura of culinary austerity
is counterbalanced by its sonic piquancy
sliced prepares the mind with a clean sinuous line
raw opens the maw
red build alliteratively upon raw's r and together
the two words, red and raw,
evoke an embodied irritation that onion undercuts
on is so short, so ordinary, so serviceable that its own mystery—

the way establishes a spatial relationship of contiguity
and priority between any two things—
might well have been ignored.
I'm always afraid I won't be understood, which spurs
my propensity towards overexplaining myself, but as a challenge
to myself, and a gift for you, I leave you pumpernickel
with its dark grainy pleasures, unexplained

Ordinary Water

for Kelley Roberts

A house's water is measured out with cups
to quench ordinary thirst
showers to lave the body
a stoppered tub filled with suds
(is an ordinary extravagance I enjoy without compunction)
to wash plates and carry away waste
A house is confronted with water externally
drizzled on or drubbed with tropic thunder
insinuating itself in through cracks or
harbored invisibly in the air itself as humidity
Comingling with dirt it makes mud
which, tracked in, gives its moisture
up to the air and down to the floor
binding to it and inviting the attentions
of the mopping subject
When you're mopping and you get the floor a little too wet
and you have to really wring the mop
dry enough to sop
up the excess water
back into its strands
back into the bucket
leaving a glistening layer
but not so wet that it'll take forever to dry
and you had really put your back into it

so when you stand up you can feel it
both the bending and the pushing
and the aftermath of an exertion
beyond the less calisthenic task, like,
watering the plants
though you can be too liberal in your ministrations
pouring water until it doesn't merely darken the soil
but courses past the roots
and flows out the holes at the base
water spilling over the lip of the saucer
on which the pot rests
onto the wood of the bookshelf
threatening the family portrait
and the books beneath
You don't wash books with water
unless they get some schmutz on their glossy covers
but even then you go gingerly
moistening a tea towel or a washcloth
gently rubbing it clean and drying it after

PowerXtreme

for Patty Gone

Any old thing
you sure do
Mama with a long-A
Mumma with a u

lickety split
spit mixed with clay
what strange cravings
my mouth tenses with my shoulders
a cavalcade of new dots on my arms
bc I've been 'forgetting' to wear sunscreen—
don't tell mama

baby in a bassinet
kitten in the crèche
tipping over the plastic accoutrements
illuminated from within by electric bulbs

my former messiah seems
vague and out-of-touch
dusty ornamental
and a bon Christmas repast
ham green beans and potatoes au gratin
it's plastic links us all

that's my oceanic feeling
(see Pinar Yoldas and Jen Scappettone)
asking all of y'all what dolls you had,
action figures

Today I remember
it was my birthday
driving to the same mall
where I saw *The Little Mermaid*
and one of my parents ran in
(it was raining heavily in San Antonio)
and got me one of the Centurions
his full mustache, the green and black of his exo-frame suit
pointless now

His name was Max. Max Ray.

What's happening in the troposphere

for Claire Hawley Crews

There's an air force base
near Western MA
sometimes the big carrier planes fly by
bellies big with weapons, bodies, fuel, who knows what else?

I don't know and they don't tell me!
I'm a civilian, ma, that's what I've been trying to tell you.
I paid $200 not to fight in the civil war
that's not true—actually I was born in 1984 or 1988
I can't remember.

She's having a baby, a hopeful future noncombatant
apple sauce in a jar, I want to teach them Spanish, Ladino,
Catalan, Occitan, kindness, Arabic, French,
ancient Greek, Italian, Cantonese, sharing, Nahuatl,
and Maltese, the only Semitic language which is an official
language of the EU, cooperation, Eastern Songhay,
Bengali, and BCS (Bosnian-Croatian-Serbian)

Sometimes a sonic boom, I still turn my head up for it
but I know I'll see nothing—and it's true! I see nothing
all the stupid planes are expensive and the supersonic
ones are probably extra expensive.
It galls me. God, nations are dumb.

Are we done yet?

I want to teach them stellar cartography, guerilla librarianship,
magic, reverie, a sort of loose taxonomic structure for states of being,
humor, and abhorrence of violence, except in resistance
to oppression, unable to be spelled without the word
press, like the sky presses down upon us

These things coexist, military planes and my dreams for a future
        child,
but I can't synthesize them. They coexist uneasily in this poem,
as I imagine they will should that future come.

Every morning

Every morning I have my morning sneezes,
place my bare feet on the wooden floor
having worn my socks to bed and after
until my feet were so covered and so hot
that I pinched some of my left sock
between the big and middle toes of my right foot
and yanked it off. Same on the other side.

How strange it would feel
to wake up someplace other than my bed.
When I was last in New York,
I stayed for a night at Elæ's, and they insisted
I wear socks or slippers in the morning—
worried about all the heat I would lose.

In the supernatural shows I watch,
some ethereal substance—sure,
call it soul—can be magicked
out of the body. If the hero
isn't too late, the process can be stopped,
reversed, even.

Being eager, sometimes desperate,
to suspend my disbelief, it takes a deliberate
act of will to mentally edit out this purple CGI haze,

which has the effect of drawing my attention
away from where it had been directed, the liminal
space between the actors' bodies, back
to the actors themselves: the agony
of the one whose soul is slipping out or in,
the strain and focus of the one who is
magicking the life force in or out.

A little estuary

My mom and my sister were there, but I got into a big fight with
my mom and told her to leave. Even in the midst of my anger, I
knew I was acting like a total ass.

My sister left, too.

I told Ell, "I don't want to keep coming to the end of the day
and numbing myself."

Around the block, walking where people aren't meant to walk,
Patsy tucked under my left arm like a football.

Last night I dreamt—

but what does it matter to you?

The task of the poem is to make it matter, and I can already tell that
    I have failed,
with the wobbly motor skills; mainly business, not residential.

At some point in the dream, my friend who moved away

soon she started having some kind of allergic reaction
presumably to the chicken which had been seasoned with

the slowness with which I often move in dreams.

I went back into my new apartment building, circa 2009,
where I was briefly a tech worker's bohemian window dressing
but then as she got worse, I decided to stop drinking.

The 'plot' never resolved, it closed at five,
like everything else in the neighborhood

No Benadryl to give to her
around the block only the smooth façade of the opera house,
and an overpass under which was something like a little estuary,
brackish and partially enclosed, in which algae bloomed
and sand glinted, in the places where the sun touched it
through the water.

My opposites

after Rachel Corbett's You Must Change Your Life: The Story of
Rainer Maria Rilke and Auguste Rodin

Like Rainer Rilke,
whom, like his mother Phia,
I prefer to call "Sophie"
I think of myself
as a person who gets sick a lot
and is given to airy sentiments

who, like many,
at some point
in her early career
(Definition 2: "to go at top speed especially in a headlong manner"
but less the top speed
and more the headlong manner)
has also made the mistake

of waiting to be inspired,

I feel like I can understand
the magnitude of having
handicraft
modeled
by a 'workmanlike' artist
like Rodin:

the double gift
of seeing touchingly
and working steadily
(the antonym of Mercury)

About the exchange between these artists
 Lou Andreas-Salomé approvingly said,
"That you gave yourself to your opposite,
your complement,
to a longed-for exemplar—
gave yourself the way one gives oneself in marriage—.
 I don't know how else to express it,
—there is for me a feeling of betrothal in this book,
—of a sacred dialogue,
 of being admitted into what one was not but now, in a mystery, has
      become,"

My mentorships and collaborations have sometimes been vexed
my opposites have moved to opposite ends of the country
or the globe

I theorize that
if I had the strength to go into the void
and through it

I would meet myself as an other
and love her

No sunlight

Salt, sweet, fat.
I don't care about a "Christmas star"
Charlotte sends me an article about the Pinkertons
and robber baron Bezos

I want to organize with Lucy Parsons in Chicago
and discuss new developments
in psychology and aesthetics
with the Munich phenomenologists

to ask Hannah Arendt if
the Vita Activa and the Vita Contemplativa
are really opposed
but I'd be embarrassed to ask
before I've finished her book

Last night I lay on the couch
and watched Jos Charles's talk
on lyric something-or-other
at the Poetry Project

cravenly jealous of trans
academic stars

even though talking with Zach earlier had made me remember

that I don't want to be famous, just 'part of the conversation'
(I'm not sure why that bit needs scare quotes)

but despite my resolve not to become bitter
I am, occasionally, a little bitter

and in those moments, I become
not the public intellectual I fantasize about being

but just someone who couldn't hack it

in bed, in pain
no sunlight
no pizza

Daily Poem

It got easier
like the word milk
but not the substance

my boohoos went by the wayside
the class went into a supernumerary session
all for the pleasure of each other's company

B visited me on the couch and
we had an important conversation

I finished the book I was reading

a wintry mix fell on Northampton

Amanda called me and we talked while cooking dinner

Britt wrapped Patsy in her coat
(marsupial mama)
and she fell asleep there

while we watched *Dawson's Creek*

This is a true and honest account of my day,
Saturday, 5 December 2020.

In the bath I didn't take

India is having a massive general strike
and we've got bupkis

"Well," I want to say to myself,
"that's not entirely true…"
We have
a thousand little points of light
they're just not quilted yet,
like the disparate elements of this poem
in which a computer's bad bit
has nothing to do with the vagaries
of group dynamics or with

December, 2011,
when we shut down the Port of Oakland

In the bath I didn't take
I was going to read Barbara Guest
but instead I drank draughts of tea
while doing my night dishes
old episodes of "Community" in the background

If you provide the space
you are in some way responsible
for what happens within it

its microagressions and scandals

wanting it to be a just and gentle place
and at the same time characterized by divagation

come on, y'all, let's divagate

People used to say some computers had a bad bit
maybe a problem with the motherboard

My parents let me take some devices apart
probably crossing their fingers that I would be
one of those little savants who could put them back together

but, alas, I proved more adept at dismantling
than remantling

glitchy patterns pop momentarily
square textured patches of visual error

Epistolary

Amy says the reason why my previous series of poems really
    popped
was the fact that they were addressed to specific people, so:

Dear Santa,

I need to make like $1,000
this month and I do not know where it is coming from.

Will I be able to launch another class?

Swinging from vine to vine—is that really a thing?

I have
mad love
for Brendan Fraser,
star of 1997's *George of the Jungle*,
based on the 1967 cartoon series,

1992's *Encino Man*,
which I learn from Wikipedia
was "known as *California Man* in France, Great Britain, Asia, and
    New Zealand,"

and of course,

1999's *The Mummy*.

I was up all night ruminating,
instead of being rocked in the strong yet gentle arms
of Brendan Fraser's oneiric double.

Sore at the joints and fully aware of the structural reasons or
      whatever,

I kept hitting "extend sleep timer" on the audiobook of Agatha
Christie's 1922 novel *The Secret Adversary*, in which Tommy and
Tuppence, who I describe to Britt as sidekicks ("You mean like they
are both sidekicks of someone else, or just each other's sidekicks?"
"Each other's!"), decide to become adventurers,

since it's after the Great War
and jobs are scarce,

and are rapidly embroiled in a mystery with larger geopolitical
      implications.

Oh, Santa, Santa, forgive me! How quickly this poem stopped
being a letter to you and became a vehicle to seek the laughter and
sympathy of others...

Who are you though?

Your temporality is complex in that you are often conjured
through the trope of adult disbelief

which is discovered to conceal childhood belief
repudiated yet now recovered
through imaginative re-investment
in childhood as the proper time of belief

et cetera!

This particular nostalgia, shared by
Edward Eager,
JM Barrie,
AA Milne,
et al.

absorbed by actual children
who will later say:

"I was nostalgic from a very early age."

Exit

The first time I ever tried to sing karaoke
it was some hipster thing
both in the sense that hipster
was a charge more frequently levied at the time
and in that the songbook had Le Tigre
whose "My Metrocard" I signed up to sing
forgetting, in a trans kind of way,
that I am more of a baritone
and that if I want to sing Le Tigre
I need to be clear about how I will shift it to my range
but I hadn't learned that lesson yet
I squeaked and ran off stage
I went with one of my exes—
she was next. I stayed outside
while she sang.
I want to say the song was Heart's "Crazy on You"
She shredded. Of course she did!
This ex had an annoying habit of being good at everything,
but it wasn't right not to come back,
sit down, and celebrate her pipes,
and later she let me know it.

Poem for Hoa

Dear Hoa,

Although I believe you favor the Mythic Tarot these days,
you were using the Barbara G. Walker tarot deck when we met
so that was what I started with:

> Nimue ordering the elements
> Attargatis' beehive pate

from 15 until 35
when my best friend was leaving the country
and I couldn't think of anything big enough
and small enough for her suitcase
except for this

These days I use the Illuminated Tarot
from which I pull a card for you:
the five of cups

Five chalices with flowers, four of which are toppled
and one still standing

the book says, "learning from mistakes" and "moving forward"
but the routes of time and growth are circuitous,
labyrinthine, even.

They double back to when I was
standing by your chimenea,
shredding the label on a bottle of beer
while I talked to you or Dale, or Philip
Sharon, RJ, Denise, Scott, Peggy Kelly,
Susan, Farid

though these names, like the decks above,
are minor arcana for other readers

Thank you for being my teacher
and an anchor during some of my most chaotic years

I'm sorry I hung around for so long
10 years off and on until I finally managed
to leave Austin

I was going to say "achieved escape velocity"
and my friend likes when I say things like that,
like when they are caught in a negative line of thought
I say, "Pull up!"

but I didn't want you to think your mentorship was something to
    escape

I was a big hormone
restive
sleepy

sitting on your grey sectional
Philip's painting hanging above it
a shimmering transdimensional portal
smack dab in the middle of Titania and Oberon's wood

smoking a cigarette on your porch
nettle tea, sweet potatoes in a pyrex pan lined with parchment
    paper,
running around after Way and K
a mentor is an oracle
an arbiter
a ground for the work of differentiation

Smol Bean

Keep going as best I can
despite the fact that the line—
and children, won't someone think
of the children?

Little word-children whose sweaters are the extra syllables
I told them to wear because I simply can't afford to keep
the house hot enough for plain language

Language, that proxy for touch in the erotics of friendship.

The heat clicks, an adjustment of the floorboards with respect
to a reluctant Humphrey Bogart finally deciding to grow a spine
and support the French Resistance
                                    but not Humphrey Bogart,
no, the character he plays—who can remember his name?

A letter says this: I give you a moment of my life, like that Ray
Bradbury Halloween book where all the kids shave a year each
off the end of their lives for their friend

for their friend

for my friend…what wouldn't I give for my friend?
Patience, and tame the volatility of my melodrama

no ocean floors   no empire state buildings

someone who understands that my lapses into high-flown
diction are, well…

My language says I'm proud
and self-conscious.

My language wants to be perceived as strange by many
but by some as not merely peculiar but peculiarly beautiful

like
What are you into?

baroque
excessive
mannered
affected
but also:
a smol bean
the uwu emoji
claimed by memes to be beloved by bottoms

Was Bogey a bottom?
Bacall a top?

a schematic translucency flopped onto a cell of film
in a dark room whose inhabitants have been lulled
into a hypnogogic state by the heat and the hum
of the projector

Dear Diary

Dear Diary,

When you have something happen
hermetically closed-off from the rest of your life
who can you talk to about it?

I guess I have therapy tomorrow.

I guess the snow protects the wood louse.

I guess I could just tell you about it,
or talk around it.

I did the food deliveries on Tuesday:
nine between Springfield, Northampton,
and Florence—it would have been ten
but there was one address that didn't exist
and Caleb couldn't figure it out either so,
because it was below freezing,
I decided to keep the box in my trunk for now.

Like the last delivery day, I found myself
listening to Liz Phair, but this time
it was the song "Polyester Bride" on repeat

because the melody has a pleasing shape,
because I like the timbre of Liz Phair's voice,
and because I can project myself into the scene
me, a complicated woman, and my bartending friend,
Henry, telling me I've got beautiful eyes,
telling me I've got time,

except for the ride from Springfield back to Northampton
when Art called me, and we talked for a while.

His questions can sometimes be so rapid
(not aggressive, but curious, enthusiastic)
that it's hard to ask him about his life
and I wonder if this is a defense
so what if it is?

Aren't we entitled to defend
the squishy inner parts of us
as best we can?

I want my friends to feel safe
within themselves
and safe with me

opening ourselves up as much as we possibly can
and not a micron further

Mouthfeel

"Mutualist usufruct" is a pretty phrase
that I learned from the Wikipedia article
on "Anarchist Economics"

Mutualism makes a kind of intuitive sense to me:
mutual aid, mutually beneficial. It's lateral, encompasses
everyone involved. Interesting to note that it features
a vowel-consonant-vowel pattern that also shows up in usufruct:
u-t-u precedes, prefigures, u-s-u

Usufruct, I had to look up, but before I tell you
what it means (if you didn't happen to know already)
would you consent to tarry with me in the mouthfeel of this word?

Eww mouthfeel, someone is saying, and yes, I guess, it could be
     gross,
but would you deny the pleasure in running the mouth through its
     courses
in the process of making the shapes to say the many names of god
(every arbitrary sign)?

Usu- and the lips tighten and extend slightly
and anyway, U is kind of a bedroom vowel,
the sound of a grand conjunction.
U is like "Oo, baby I love your ways"

and it even means union in maths,
but this union is deferred by the sibilance of the S,

as if UU is a field of Gazing Grain
and S is the snake passing through it,
Death's Carriage

Perhaps the Gazing Grain is a fruited plain
F for fullness, R for ripe, U we have already established
is the cleave the crack the space between the toes
of the word where the tongue goes

and weirdly, I intuited the onomatopoeia of this word,
which (sorry not sorry for having withheld it this long) refers to the
"right to the use and profits of the property of another without
     damaging it"
from the Latin *usus et fructus*, use and enjoyment

Chassis

Wake up, make coffee, blow my nose a thousand times, read an article about socialist Yugoslavia's DIY home computing craze in the 80s, read a text from EH from last night—they are sad about not getting the Hampshire job, a fog hangs over the land like a moist exhalation in a cold, unventilated room. The repair people Kathy hired are working outside the bedroom window, so I put some pants on. I receive a text from a 512 number (Austin, where I was born). It reads, "chassis down alarms," and it becomes a leitmotif in my morning conversation with B. I receive a call from the same number, "Is this Nick?" "No, I think you have a wrong number" Who even answers anymore when a strange number calls? I guess I'm looking for something to happen. What do I think this is, a Murakami novel? That I haven't read one in years doesn't make the image less present to me: a kind of blank everyman cooking pasta and listening to Rossini's "Thieving Magpie" when a mysterious woman calls. Add this to the file of things I want to read, but gay. Her name is Chassis Down and what she has to say will alarm you.

A boring poem

For Katy Burnett

The X-Files episode "Ice,"
first aired on November 5, 1993,
(a year after *Twin Peaks: Fire Walk With Me*)
finds Mulder and Scully
trapped in an Antarctic
research station with two scientists
the pilot who flew them there
a dog
and the bodies
of the researchers
they have come to investigate
who were killed by a parasite
unearthed by boring into the ice shelf
which I remembered as a being a
Real Science Thing, confirmed
by a quick looksee at the NSF's
Ice Core Facility website:
"By drilling down into the ice sheet or glacier
and recovering ice from ancient times,
scientists are able to determine the past composition
 and behavior of the atmosphere,
what the climate was like when the snow fell,
and how the size of ice sheets and glaciers have changed
in the past in response to different climate conditions."

Composition, or,
what you are made of,
and behavior, or,

behavior

We all have a personal mythology:
this is how it began   this
is what happened next   I thought
I was…

All Mulder is really asking is that Scully
entertain a willingness to consider explanations
ordinarily dismissed out of hand as impossible

All Scully is really asking is for Mulder
not to always turn to aliens
as the first or most likely explanation

I thought I was going to be telling a story of 2008—
the history of exes can be lively and fun in the retelling
and the retelling of one's personal mythology
is a foundational gesture of friendship

and yet,
in the glint of the sun on the ice
that forms the crust on this poem
I feel compelled to bore more deeply

and, as with the unmelted ice, back in time
to my teenage years and thus
to the origin of the coping mechanism

not that interesting: it was a chaotic era
and I turned to dating as something close,
comprehensible, a way to make something
fucking happen in the world albeit
not predicated on achieving anything

perfect for a dropout like me
and antithetical, one might say, to
rising through the ranks of the Vancouver
comedy scene before moving to LA
presumably for the opportunities
only to come to the attention of Judd Apatow

The rest, as they say, is history,
departing from LA for SF
a site of continued shenanigans
but also of the slow and at times
recidivist progress towards filling
my inner emptiness
with the person I have become

Janáček's Enigmatic Tones

For Bethany Ides and Ora Ferdman

Dear Castrato Cantata Cantina,

who remind me of the various strategies
through which we can resist the wolfish
violence of incorporation

Castrati as such
are mostly from another era
and this is one strategy (time travel)

some chose to be
others didn't—

—this wasn't strategy
but we can use it

obliquity
opacity
resistance to naming
the traumas they've experienced
(continue to experience)

difference-in-multiplicity

calling the university to
instantiate
in the bodies of its representatives

for those representatives
who typically hide behind a parclose screen
to see what it's like to be called
to sing and show their bodies

I'm doing too many projects
like Kirk from *Gilmore Girls*

existential loneliness can be present
even if you are surrounded by friends
that is, in a 2020 kind of way
(that is, one at a time)

I was looking at the twitter of a writer I like
and now I'm listening to the piano music of Leoš Janáček

I'm sick of the I
I wish I could just write about mythological and historical themes
the succulence of objects in the specificity
of how they object to nothingness

why can't you?

the wind is in me

I walk the overgrown path

I approach the flames as if they would burn me
and they do burn me

would you stay in hell if all your friends were there?

outside the fire's sphere of influence
is a colder darker world

you could stumble and fall
becoming plant food

I'm sick of the I
sick of this country
sick of English

I can't very well go to the mountains can I
to reinvent the steam engine

then I would really be alone

I'm definitely sick of the internet
of which I have the impression
that it was once somewhat charming and experimental
(vestiges remain)
the personal websites of the geocities archive, etc.

twitter makes me feel so damn lonely
I'm not as snarky as the other trans girls, mama
and although we all seem to know
it's the psychological architecture
of that built environment,
which arouses controversy
fuels and foregrounds it
we're all still there

But it must be said that Bethany invited me to
Investigative Operatics
where I get to meet new people
visit a corner of the creative world I don't live in

and Janáček plays the seven noble chords
not disdaining to build a staircase and walk us up and down it
with enigmatic tones as well

Dear LL and VS

Dear LL and VS,

I'm sorry I was so quiet
in our writing group last night
I was feeling kind of like I didn't belong
my brain is fuzzier in the evenings
and everyone there is so smart
and knowledgeable
so good at giving constructive criticism
(while I am secretly very first thought, best thought)

I feel connected enough to the threads of
my old community in the Bay to understand
where you are coming from
I mean like a matrix of writers artists activists
to situate your work within
and the way some of those people
have been influenced by New Narrative
as well as the ways that New Narrative writers
have really been taken up by folks
as a way of feeling historical
I mean like of wanting something particular from history

I hope it doesn't seem like I'm being critical of this impulse
just that I wanted to talk about how

to seek out find document publish write about a movement
is also to construct it
a creative act
and a testament to how
ancestors not only create us
we create them

but I am not connected to the living ongoing reality

after the fire

after the fires

after the days of orange sky

after the completion of the salesforce tower
or the addition of new BART stops
or whatever new ads are up around town,
though I ask Amy to tell me about them

I'm touched to still be as folded in as I am—
showing up with Sam as the "Northampton contingent"
mentioned in Noah's "Diary of a Bookseller"

And now the pandemic is on and suddenly
by virtue of this and my other writing group
I am more in California than I have been since May of 2016
when we drove across the continent

to make a new life here
that started with grad school
which I hated
but which was the center of gravity of my community here
such that I'm still living in its aftermath

Monday and Tuesday nights,
I'm happy to be with my distant friends
who are talented writers and thinkers
people I care about

but whose existence
both in itself
and in relation
(to each other, to the place)
refutes something I have needed to believe:

that we got out while the getting was good
that Oakland is *over*
in the way that my parents
felt like the Austin of the 70s and 80s
didn't exist anymore
or how Hoa and Dale talked about San Francisco
where they had gone to grad school at New College (like Carrie)
which doesn't exist anymore

Notley writes:

> I am still with you in that
> part of the
> park, and vice will continue, but
> I'll have
> a cleaning Maine.

and I do have a cleaning Maine, so to speak:
the trees scrub the air
and swathe the bears in needed shadow.

They harbor the deer who harbor the ticks
who carry some nasty diseases

I think about my night runs ten eleven years ago
the chill fog beading into droplets on my glasses
my rule for myself that if I came to a fork in the road
I would take the steeper path
an entity alone I've never felt stronger
enjoying my post-run cigarette

My back hurts like hell today and getting older has unfortunately
not come with an attendant increase in earning power or
    subcultural status
but Diane di Prima prepared me for this.

I want to find the center of gravity
for the poetry community here

the publications the gathering spaces
but I also know it's not something you find
or not completely rather, it's something you build together

and it has vice in it, too
it can't help but have

[this isn't done, but I had to stop writing and start working]

Thanatopsis

the pirate's cove

recondite library

unseelie court of readers

coffee mother cave

illicit lesbianic grove of secrets

the shadow glimmer

Weimar club in the cinematic imaginary—dark

Placid lake surface concealing concrete cold war bunker, now
unused

fat veil

hermetic eyrie

occult convention center

invisible tree house

inside the human suit

Thanatopsis Written Using Generative Techniques of Karinne Keithley Syers

the pirate's cove was a stupid name
for a secret meeting place, a clubhouse, really
it sounds like a bougie snack
or a filesharing website
but it was actually a really cool place
my friend built from scrap lumber
near their house
with a French drain snaking
around the sides so that a heavy rain
wouldn't set it tumbling down the hillside

because they lived in Cummington
which was the childhood home of William Cullen Bryant
to obtain entry
you had to memorize his poem
"Thanatopsis"
from Greek *Thanatos* (death) and *opsis* (view, sight)
This poem was actually memorized by generations of
US school-children, which was just the sort of antiquarian
touch that would appeal to Veronica

it's about death
taking comfort in Nature

(and Bryant was writing in the heyday
of the capitalization of this word,
the anti- or ante-deity of the Transcendentalists)
Communion with Nature, Bryant argues,
will lead you, organically, as we might say today,
to contemplation of the universality of the thing
Death I mean
If you ask the dead
"When will I see you again?"
(The Three Degrees' exquisite plaint)
you'll get no answer
I resolve not to dwell on death today—
my friends', my own—
but rather the silences, absences, distances,
which are, theoretically, revocable

A little pile

Woke up late with Patsy curled in my armpit
things are still blech
even though she smells like a little Frito
I scooch her little body over
so I can sit up with my computer
sipping coffee and writing my daily poem
I've been letting the work pile up for a day or two
like an actor asking *what's my motivation?*
money you dingdong
you have to keep earning it
and fighting about it
indefinitely
unless you figure out
a better way to communicate about it
and unless we (the big we, society)
manages to enact a better system
for the distribution of goods
and opportunities
and yes there are ways
to prefiguratively enact
other ways of doing things
but money is still a dwelling
health insurance
food
and more complicated things

like the imperative to be an instance

though asking we, money communicates it
and dingdong
you're it

indefinitely
I in poem
I've blech
even things
like imperative things
but ways
to with
ways of about
little ways

and society
manages body
my armpit
things distribute

prefiguratively earning my system
for to be a work-her
still a figure yes there for goods
and my curled indwelling
health instance

about with us two
like, big are
the opportunities
and in doing so enact
other computers

sipping like coffee
unless December
still the better or an actor
more keep you complicated to scooch
fighting enact is we I and Patsy
up my what's way she over
so daily ways
the smells
writing day motivation?

money have
unless up been it
and insurance
food
can are better
and 2020 woke
up late
letting out a little pile
of sit you up

Your valid extended play remix

Written this way, your is possessive

the engine of the lyric poem for me is longing

"if your [sic] vaccinated spit in my mouth"

vowels as slippery as a muff
in the capable hands of Eleanor Roosevelt
U that sounds—almost—like O, etc.
and the great northern vowel shift
in the mouth of my midwestern lady hubby

the snow falls fleet and fulsome outside
but we are out of oil today
one space heater runs in the living room
and another in the bedroom

Sic means thus
and *cum* means with

"Come my lady / come, come my lady / you're my butterfly / sugar
    / baby"
by Crazy Town, release date October 26, 1999

I spent the morning listening to recordings of Akilah Oliver
    readings on PennSound

the oldest is the Belladonna* one from 1999.

For reference, I was 15, we had just moved from Dallas to Austin
and all I knew of poetry was
Gilgamesh, Beowulf, The Odyssey
ee cummings to whom Kalmia had introduced me
was the closest thing to a living poet I knew
and he had died in 1962

Possible that someone heard that silly Crazy Town song on the
radio on the way to the reading
and it was still jangling around in their head and tension in their
body from the journey to the reading and stimulation from the
social element of the reading flirting and schmoozing or studiously
avoiding their nemeses and exes settling in the folding chairs until
the reading begins and something in the body settles and shifts

the doors of perception
aka the body
are flung open

At least that's how these things go or used to go

I am not there
I am not then

I am inside my house where these days I mostly always am
In my 'real life' this morning I
listened to a Youtube playlist

that Karen from Investigative Operatics sent me
"Your tewnty [sic] favourite hiphop nostalgia tunes"
with Timbaland, Aaliyah, etc.
drank coffee
ate my oatmeal
I sent the playlist to Lindsay because I knew she would like it

Texted Britt to say I know somebody who knows their cousin
and that I want to kiss them (Britt)
on the lips

with tongue

Ell texted to ask what that journal was called, but I didn't
    remember

Jina's cats are at the vet but it's just for a routine checkup thank
    goodness

fuck this is just a list now not a poem

I feel cold
I feel itchy in my soul

I feel suspicious of the tyranny of two
but also like I belong in it
I wanna be public-facing
but instead I'm just you-facing

The Fence

No more big personalities!

I am a field of wildflowers
and you are a trampling bull
or at least that's how it feels sometimes

Is it stupid to ask for the revolution to include some level of
emotional self-awareness?

Otherwise traumatized people will keep traumatizing each other
and as concrete is poured over a lattice of rebar
but...this simile doesn't make sense
because rebar helps strengthen concrete under tension
whereas...

Every time my throat hurts
I want to say the word like "thwoat"
but some people do not find this cute

I thought it was Friday for a second
shirking my paid duties as long as I can
in order to get a mental hit
is not my preference just something that happens

shoutout to my fellow procrastinators

suddenly quitting or pausing all my Zooms
a proprietary video conferencing software
that many of us were using during the pandemic of 2020-?
(she explained, in a burst of optimism looking forward to a time
when even the terrible or seemingly all-encompassing things of the
     present
will need footnoting)

what if I just want to write and for that to be the job
some writer-friends say they prefer to keep their creative activities
at a remove from their wage labor

but I'm in the faction that has embraced the entanglement
like a vanguardist? no, a nostalgic
who wants never to have been anything
other than a poet
"and all her ancillary activities have been directed to that end"
as Alice Notley's bio says

In practice this life is characterized by constant turmoil
and ethical calculations

it's just that I don't really believe it is possible to circumvent these
     things

I hate it when people aren't self-aware enough to realize how
     thoroughly they have trampled my clover

but somehow or other
a bull keeps getting through the fence

probably because I keep letting them through

Well-known eccentrics

"Your Pattern
It's possible that you're taken for granted, used,
or even mistreated. Instead of backing off and…"

but the notification cuts off there

later I'll open and know what I should do instead

of smoking copiously in my dreams and memories
Lucky Strikes Camel Lights Skydancers Pall Malls and that blue
    pouch for rollies
through which, among other methods, ~I~ was the mistreater
in retrospect my death drive was lavish and robust

I'm trying to find them on the maps

the places where I used to wander

I'm remembering to say gwahduhloop and maynor
so when I go home I don't seem like a fool
who doesn't remember where she's from

Home is when you feel situated in a place
even if you don't ultimately feel like you belong there, like: it was
my role to drink a black coffee and read and smoke on the patio at

Spider House on Fruth and live my teenage/early 20s life while my
mom worked at the school in the old women's dorm up the block

thinking about the first trans woman I ever knowingly saw

Jennifer Gale
from her Wikipedia page:

"Gale was one of a number of well-known Austin eccentrics which
include urban outdoorsman cross-dresser Leslie Cochran, who also
had run for municipal office in Austin, Texas."

If you click eccentric, the wiki authors mention "unusual or
odd behavior" but aver that, "This behavior would typically be
perceived as unusual or unnecessary, without being demonstrably
maladaptive."

I assumed that if I had stayed in Austin, I would've remained
under the sign of the eccentric, at best

and a poet not a musician a double oddity
Embarrassing to admit that I just wanted to go somewhere and be
if not normal
then in context

Well now you are and how do you like that

how do you like that

The Painting of My Life

Begin exiting from a dream in which
the rungs of the ladder were breaking under me
and then
the dawn
you said you saw my finger twitch
saw me press my pelvis to the archive
but on the other hand you believe
that we awaken out of nothing

Grimacing at the emergency's seemingly
endless encores
I dreamed, wakefully now, that I was
in the studios of Paris in the 1950s
or synchronized swimming
just one of the myriad Nereids

Not one of the peoples of the corn—
the crust of colonialism has jagged edges

Maybe the way to enter the day would be reading aloud
although no one else is here today besides the dog
limiting the opportunity for unmediated conversation
at this time
tho, it must be said, she responds in her way and
recognizes quite a few English phrases

and many more embodied and olfactory cues

I just wanted something to ensue
so I went to the painting of my life given to me by my memories
in which everything that happened is still moving
to plumb the joys of known affinities

and then I went to Facebook where someone
articulates a radical vision

maddening because I know they'll soon be yelling at me

what's radical about that?

La la la

slugabed
coffee
Patsy in the fold
I want a pastry

what do I write about
la la la

Supposed to walk with Charlotte in an hour
I need to shave and do something with my hair

once again I went to that strange city I go to in my dreams
where I will go when I am dead (?)

the she said dialogues: flesh memory bibliomancy:
Oliver writes, "catching the wet doubts so sweet."

The image for February is a set of undulant parallel grooves
like a close-up of corduroy
or the impression corduroy makes on soft skin

like ripples in a pond, I want to write,
but do ripples ever bend
almost into a row of esses like that?

I was supposed to wash something we were planning to eat later
in the toilet, and even in the dream this seemed disgusting
but I was doing it

Alternative Poetry

Lunch with Francis on Friday
we drove the swaying road to South Hadley
past the red schoolhouse and the markers
of the 1936 flood
to Duro West African Cuisine
to get some jollof and plantains

I'm about to quit Spotify
it's always the same with tech:
they hate workers and love surveillance
but that day
the algorithm made me a station
out of "Need You Around"
by Smoking Popes

("What genre is that?" Amy asks
"The album is born to quit from 1995…
what genre? I'm like: is this alternative music?")

Is there such a thing as alternative poetry?
I pull Daniel Davidson's *Culture* from the shelf and give it a flip:

Even and embroiled in implication, so disturbs the ghost of empire ...
        behavior of empirical. Return to the semblance of fact
            X of memory, fortune and control ...

a receipt from Blick and a booking confirmation for a flight from SF
 to Boston
ida y vuelta

On the ride home the person from the restaurant
calls back to apologize for giving Francis goat—
"Don't be mad at me," they said in the message,
not knowing that Francis would never.

Driving past New England farms and their farmhouses
into denser neighborhoods with houses
I couldn't yet identify as Eastern Stick or Italianate
Nerf Herder's "Van Halen" plays
off their 1996 self-titled album

in which they sing:
"Tomorrow may come / tomorrow may never come"

I don't want to live in the world that produced these songs
I already did

I don't want to be 12 again
and powerless

It's just that I was 12 in 1996 and no other year
I wasn't 12 in 1975 or 2010, okay?
I don't want to be 12 again
but I do feel myself regressing—

fascism / pandemic n'est-ce pas?

—and I try to keep it contained
in my media
rather than my behavior

In my dream, I wasn't wearing my glasses
like most of yesterday
and I saw Becca in the distance
in front of a golden sunset

Becca and Ell when we used to jam
did they know it was wringing from the past
it's terrible power?

that singing those songs with confidence
I became an agent?

Being alive

Warm air blows from the vent on the floor
into the red shirt hanging from the curtain rod
filling it up and making it dance like there's a woman inside

Thinking of the phrase
"waiting in death's vestibule"
as a way to say
"being alive"

where is the soul?
it is filling up the windsock

With a mouth full of toes
I admire your muscular calves
and big thighs

I whisk
and
you thicken

when it's my turn
I find I am pulling your hand
a little too hard into my pussy—sorry!

Is ecstasy the only thing with throes?

Dragging My Feet

back into to the sea
back into the seeming

I'm dragging my feet about this thing I said I'd write
won't someone help me figure out why?

Listening to sea oleena's "Weaving a Basket" but I'm not going to
go on about it like I usually do

Zoom meeting about a potential gig today
try not to seem too desperate

bust darts
plant shadows

I'm the mother of things that are able to cry out

*everything I can hear cry out

Britt says that I'm an archaeologist
and I know what they mean but I pretend
that I don't because I want to hear
how they would explain it

My job is to sing, goddammit, to sing!

I was never issued a physical insurance card!

Why aren't I better at life right now?

Well, in the past year
your body was occupied by a goa'uld
your consciousness was downloaded into a computer
and then back into your body

and that's just for starters

breathy vocals
ambient recording of wind, surf, the odd car or voice
and guitar strummed in a waltz rhythm but slow

fucking hell I wasn't going to talk about the music

I was just going to make it

Simone Weil says the truth of life on earth is force

and there is something uncrushable in me, sure

but why shouldn't I elegize the fragile parts

and the luxury of having borne them

A Poem About Simone Weil

We were looking for something five fathoms deep
but the pressure was getting to me

I'm not a field agent I'm a lurker in libraries

Is it fundamentally conservative to undertake
to preserve the arcana of the Bogomils
and the Cathars

Simone Weil loves patriotism
and Christianity in a way that's difficult for me
to understand

but I love what she says about history
being a record of the victors, which
admittedly is a commonplace but

she really digs into it, asking
what is admirable about slave-owning Romans?

Decrying our devotion to greatness
in favor of goodness

which she applies a little trans-historically
for contemporary tastes, although she does allow

that the cultural context must be considered
if not in the way that we do it

I guess the patriotism thing makes more sense if you know
she's writing from London while France, her home,
is occupied by Germany

she keeps talking about pre-Roman Gaul

A Little Sparrow

For Sophia Dahlin who got me thinking about Sappho

the edges of your blue agony
lodge less comfortably in my mommy
globules than they did in the before-times

Can't hear out of my left ear too well
can't seem to motivate myself to have
my eyes checked so I can buy glasses
with lenses that aren't scratched all to hell

this little nudge has me thinking about inevitable death as the
      horizon of the sensible

"okay grandma let's get you to bed"

Not to exaggerate, I mean I could see the wall-shrine of Mary when
      Ell pointed it out to me
but sometimes when the others talked, I just smiled and nodded at
      intervals
attending more carefully to the words that did come through,
      fragments, like

the verses of Sappho we have are all the verses of Sappho we have
we have no others (unless another papyrus should come to light etc)

I told my therapist that I was lonely for god

In *Decreation*, Anne Carson does this lovely reading of Sappho's
    "Fragment 31"
which, after having activated the dance of jealousy, begins a
    marvelous turn
"All is to be dared because even a person of poverty... ,"
before breaking off

Carson notes, "Sappho is believed by some historians to have been
not just a poet of love and a worshipper of Aphrodite on Lesbos
but also a priest of Aphrodite's cult and a teacher of her doctrines."

Given this possibility: "Perhaps Sappho's poem wants to teach us
something about the metaphysics or even the theology of love.
Perhaps she is posing not the usual lovesong complaint, Why don't
you love me? but a deeper spiritual question, What is it that love
dares the self to do?"

See a little straw poking out from the ruins of the temple to
    Aphrodite and in my surmisal
that it is a nest, I
become a little sparrow asking "Are you my mother"

I,
whatever I am, a bird, a woman, your human wife,
approach the ruins of the temple to Aphrodite
having been a student of longing
inimical to the sanctimony of that anointed

soi-disant messiah

anxious, to say the least, about the imperative to eat the other
(proselytize, convert) felt by his followers

ask,
"Are you my goddess?"

for whom I could become an academy
lesbians with hand-mirrors and papyri
just fucking anointing each other all day
with knowledge taking as our model
the subterranean affiliations of the trees,

the spume of the sea

Stargate Star Friend

Stargate Star Friend

We've established that
some things can pass
back and forth
through an open wormhole
like radio waves, for instance

"Are you there? Over."

We can dial your planet
and the wormhole opens,
stays open, without a hitch,
indicating that, whatever else is true,
the gate on your planet
is functioning normally

"Do you read me? Over."

Are you monitoring these transmissions?

Don't bury your gate
we can't yet reach you
at sub-light speeds

Field research

On the stated preferences of poets,
as I have heard them remarked upon,
during my tenancy among them,
ages 16-36 (current):

In the philosophy of language,
Wittgenstein

Among photographers,
Claude Cahun

Of mid-twentieth century comedians,
Lenny Bruce

Among jazz mystics,
Alice Coltrane

With respect to film,
Alain Resnais's *Last Year at Marienbad*

Between rust belt US cities,
Buffalo

Radical paragon,
Angela Davis

In painting,
it's tough to decide between Cy Twombly, Philip Guston, Joan
     Mitchell, Agnes Martin, Giorgio di Chirico, and Edward
     Hopper,
               but EVERYONE seems to like Edward Hopper

But from the category of "outsider" art,
Henry Darger

Re: ways of relating to land,
the commons

Mentioned as being specifically beloved among trans women poets,
Paul Celan

From the list of heresies,
the gnostic ones (Bogomils, Cathars, Albigensians)

In sport,
baseball

When describing relationships of spatial or ontological priority,
back of (vs "behind")

Early Hominids

I hate to be forced into anything
and yet I am very agreeable

it is very hard for me to set a boundary
when someone is not helping me meet it
from the other side

shoutout to everyone helping me
to meet boundaries from the other side

Standpoint epistemology
and the lyric I
have collided more profoundly in my
poetic practice than even I know

If your
"self-appointed"
job is to flower
and bloom
what happens
when you meet a stink bug

Even "even I" indicates
too great
a late-stage faith

in the ability of a subject
to know itself

underneath it's all sex and shadows
early hominids with rock hammers

I still cry as if it were the first
time I saw *The Land Before Time*
when I think too hard about what
we must have done to the Neanderthals

Awaiter

Sensitive to changes in pressure and temperature

When you shifted your weight, I stumbled
revealing to me that I had been leaning on you
relying on your continued
I was going to say
presence
but you haven't gone away
just left the room for a moment

For dinner, wolf spicy noodles
with enough lemongrass
to numb the interior
of my mouth
medicament for a wet hole
that feels everything

You left the room
of my being seventeen
for just a moment
to go to college or to have something
specifically yours

It's healthy to have things
that are specifically yours

I had them eventually

an identity
an industry
at length, a past

but my thing
involves expectancy
if you agree
that the work of a poet
includes waiting
and longing

for a you which is and isn't god
a you who is and isn't here

I'm a longer, an awaiter

I don't have to point out the paradox
just walk you up to it

Barking

After Elena Comay del Junco's "Cool Women"

Your silence has been observed and noted
waking up just wanting to steal back into sleep
having a letter to respond to in Spanish
calls to return etcetera
Life's pleasures taken in the wrong frame of mind
sit as heavily as lasagna in the stomach
Warm us up some 'breakfast lasagna'
my balance is poor but in 2021
I want to ride bikes again
I don't often feel like I am a total cliché
but I read the New Inquiry piece
with a sinking feeling in my gut
my seriousness is a pose
I am three years late to the party
(seven, thirty, a hundred…)
a little girl playing Susan Sontag dress-up
and incidentally, what I believed in
is in fact a terrible institution.
What does this mean about everything else in my life
to say nothing of reality at large as I perceive it?
Had what I thought of as dues-paying
merely been the visitation of abuses
by one generation upon another?
The dog upstairs barks, I'm barking, too.

I'm biting, I'm howling, I wanted the book
I have it, it's in my jaws, but it isn't mine
I tear it up, I despair it up, it *is* mine
it must be, otherwise I shouldn't
feel such license to destroy something
categorically sacred, although
if I consider it dispassionately,
I can admit the possibility that within the sacred
hovers a little chaote, in the form of a clot
or a sudden embolism

500,000 people dead of COVID in the US & I'm sorry that being on my HD tip is how I process it

Poets have a long-standing pledge
(or is it contract, covenant?)
to elegize
(or is it eulogize?)
the dead
an obligation to remind us
that many of these deaths were needless
(what constitutes a needful death?)
though their minds should crack
(our minds should crack)
and half of what leaks out
slips into the (mythopoetic) past
in what we refer to as a jellyfish moment

I ask what mythological being would you be
and Luna says a banshee
with a gray cloak
a green dress
and eyes red from weeping

I'm always thinking about Eros and Thanatos
figuring that Thanatos has his devotees

so I ally myself to the life and sap and sexy stuff
the god retconned into a child of Aphrodite

but I guess it's the Keres,
who are associated with death by disease,
the Keres, who are the children of Nyx,
and the siblings of sweet Philotes,
goddess of affection, friendship, and sex,
hater of animal sacrifice and other
life-destroying offerings

I'm not as bad as I pretended to be

Reading Soleida Ríos's *The Dirty Text*
translated by Barbara Jamison and Olivia Lott
"By the time I learned ever so slowly to speak,
I believe I had already learned incoherence…"
Deliver the food and then bring a smoothie to Lindsay
(the vaccine made her sick for a few days)
My mom saying, "Action reduces anxiety"
No cages for kids in San Antonio or anywhere
the more energy I expend being anxious about
the things I said a soft yes to but somehow
find myself unable to do, the less I have
for being part of that good mesh, the people's
and now we're going to take this apartment
but can we afford it? B brings me coffee
in the Butterfly World mug
Apropos of a conversation from weeks ago
I wake up with a possible rejoinder:
"Olson worked for the post office"
Olson?! Who am I? Contact! Contact!
Feels like a marker of a different gen
don't worry, it is mainly in poems
that I become so navel gaze-y about historicity
Who was the last stranger to touch your hand
the last friend you physically bumped into
and how fuzzy was the wool on her cardigan?

Assuming for a moment that the way poetry
arrives is neutrinos striking the pineal gland
which is not really a signal that can be interrupted
except by the workings of the other parts of the brain
the hubbub and the jingle jangle of other thoughts
feelings sense impressions proprioception
such that the process of composition is akin to
listening for a single voice in a crowded marketplace
but what if this is a terrible mistake and you tune out
the commotion and all you hear is "la la la hosanna"
I don't believe the cosmic broadcaster would bore us with pieties
Rimbaud is a gross boy; Villon, a thief; Bataille, a pervert
and all of them lead me to the red raw excellence of Kathy Acker
I'm not as bad as I pretended to be at the sleepover
sure, I gamely added comic narration to "Red Shoe Diaries"
on "Skinemax" but then I threw up in the sink of your guesthouse
and I was so embarrassed about it, I insisted that I hadn't
I mean, that you picked me up from choir practice
should have been an indication

The Women's Building

After Soleida Ríos's El Texto Sucio / The Dirty Text *(transl. Barbara Jamison and Olivia Lott)*

Cixous and Clément (transl. Betsy Wing):

> But when the sorceress is the spectacle, tracked down everywhere, forced to defend herself even if it is with somatic insensitivity. That is where the passage is completed. As long as the sorceress is still free, at the sabbat, in the forest, she is a sensitivity that is completely exposed—all open skin, natural, animal, odorous, and deliciously dirty. When she is caught, when the scene of the inquisition is formed around her, in the same way the medical scene later forms around the hysteric, she withdraws into herself, she cries, she has numb spots, she vomits. (39)

I want to go into the Women's Building. What happens inside the Women's Building? Is it where one becomes a woman, or perhaps where one might go to have their womanhood verified? Now there's a terrible thought: they'd probably ask for two forms of idea [sic], a credit card, an insurance card; in the US we have this thing called a credit score. Maybe they'd even ask me for a letter from a psychologist, or my medical doctor, proof of surgery, things like that. Thing is, I'm on hormones, have been for years, but I've never had any kind of surgery. But maybe they wouldn't ask for any such thing, maybe those things are anathema to the ethos of the Women's Building.

Anathema, ethos; phallogocentric. I think briefly of L. saying that she has intentionally de-skilled herself.

Other ways of being 'in' the Women's Building: being 'in' a friendship between women; making love like women do with each other (a kind of mirroring, S. uses the word "twincest," shocking my delicate sensibilities); comfort with ambiguity; responsibility, right or wrong, for the recreation of the world.

To the TERF, this sounds I'm sure like infiltration, but all I'm really talking about is coming home, to a category.

Find a place where they'll let you in the Women's Building. Learn from it. Become it. Become what was already in you to become. A propensity for symbolic grammar that inheres in the structure of the brain. I don't care if it's wrong.

Do cis people have to do units of, "continuing education?"

The Newly Born Woman...but I'm not newly born. I've been a woman. I don't know how long to count for. From birth, assuming a kind of pith or germ, inchoate, sleeping, and then I become conscious of it, protect it. Whom I invited inside, literally inside of my body, have swerved, for one, or wrinkled their nose, for another. Or went inside but didn't strike the mark.

The capacity to absorb blows, secrets, to agree to carry and receive my mother's lore. Or beyond my mother, my sisters, my partner (who, in any case, IDs as woman+), into a world of women.

Find a place where they'll call you a woman. Okay, San Francisco. I
 don't want to risk it otherwise.

U said that Croatia has no extradition to the US, but this isn't about
 nations.

It's about murals, and mysteries, or Mysteries. It's about the
basement of the library. Not like smuggler's tunnels, but more
metaphysical, the connection between what happens in the
basement of the library and being admitted into the Women's
Building.

The thing is that I don't mean the actual place in the Mission. Okay,
I do and I don't. Their website explains the history of the beautiful
murals on the exterior of the Building, and the services offered
therein. The Center for Sex and Culture was an actual place, too,
but that's not what I mean, or at least, not exactly.

Metaphysical buildings/non-buildings. A nonsite collection of
unreinforced masonry, subsequently retrofitted for seismic activity.
This building contains chemicals known to the State of California
to…

My idée fixe, powdered bourgeouis faces in *Celine and Julie Go
Boating*, repeating the same bourgeois scenes until the eponymous
Celine and Julie disrupt them. That something absurd between two
women can remake the word [sic]. *Heavenly Creatures*, and what
happens you punish love.

What happens when you punish love?

I would tell you, but I have to go to work.

Ars Poetica

How do you know when to lop off a line, a lock? When something
    carries over, that's
enjambment. Look, I don't know if "hemistich" is pronounced
    "hemistitch" or "hemistick,"
but I still have to wake up, put on my pants (or not), and write the
    poem.

Writhing around on the ice beside our car, I try to get the lug nuts
out, but the tool that came with the car didn't fit. Two trips to the
hardware store and I managed to get two off but stripped the rest.
I thought *if I just keep turning the wrench* but then I finally had to call
a tow truck.

Even a poetaster knows about the oblique connection between the
stuff of everyday life and the poem. Each quotidian detail isn't a
brick. Witness today! What could you build out of this? But neither
can it be omitted.

Ell asked if I really thought we'd need English teachers in a post-
apocalyptic scenario. We had just climbed up a slippery snow-
covered hill at the time, onto a ridge above the Mill River and had
no idea where we were.

Talking with my family, I propose that numbers, by themselves,
have no intrinsic existence, but my mom said, neither do words
and that was that. The thing is that poets are human, with human

entanglements. I'm playing with this idea that we are 'intelligent receivers.'

I mean, like *possessing the faculty of intelligence,* not *distinguished by extraordinary intelligence*. Maybe each detail is a dry twig gathered from the surrounding area for the purposes of starting a fire. I swore that at the end of the pandemic, you would find me dancing naked around a bonfire with my friends.

I'm trying to fold an ars poetica into these verses, portable and modular like mass-produced furniture. Scrolling through Instagram, someone points out that the capacity to like a post is a design feature, which feels both obvious and surprising. When someone takes it upon themselves to pamper the cracks between natural and naturalized; given and constructed.

The troubadour is no stranger to artifice. Do you think I was ever a real shepherdess? Lauren keeps saying that a piece of writing is 'salted' with something or 'larded' with it, which both the cook and the writer in me love. I've long felt that the discourse of courtly love (artifice) is salted (or is it larded) with something not merely entertaining.

That is, lore and arcana of a heretical doctrine, hidden in plain sight, in a poem (entertainment). Admittedly, this could simply be a romanticized take on the role of the poet, or anyone who wants to exalt herself. And I am vain, yes. Yes, I am proud, but there's something else too, that exalted thing, I can't name it, but I'll die to preserve it (or, rather, live to learn its song and pass it on to you).

Autonomous Zones

Last night I curled onto the couch with Britt
and watched *Moxie* with her

We are
the age of moms
I mean
if I had had a kid
at the age my mom had me
they would be 14 years old
and now
if a movie is meant to be watched
by kids and their parents
the parts meant for the parents
(zines, Le Tigre soundtrack)
also flatter our generational tastes

A few days earlier
Charlotte had been telling me
about her talk on the Amish
sprung, she said, from an interest
in extant autonomous zones

I would read that, I said,
a book on autonomous zones.
What are some others?

I can only think of two, she quipped,
off the top of my head:
the Amish and
a teenage girl's bedroom

I wish that
when I was a teen
I had had a teenage girl's bedroom

Elisa had a good one, with a band of collages running across each
    wall,
and three fake carrots hanging Dadaistically from her bedroom
    ceiling

I had a map of the world
hung upside down

and the poster for *Gadjo Dilo* (1997)
from a free box outside the art house theatre

Comet

For Lee Ann Brown,
first person I ever heard sing at a poetry reading
Sung*:*

The sun returns
through the green, through the green

The sun returns through the green

Even if it were your last day on Earth

The sun
returns
through
the green

Spoken:

Driving in the car yesterday,
I remembered something else
that was in my room as a teenager:
a bunch of glow-in-the-dark plastic stars
that I had stuck on my walls
with the included adhesive
mostly in vague constellatory shapes

but some in a crude comet shape,
which I regretted every time
I turned off the lights.

We're talking about teenage girl bedrooms as autonomous zones.

My bedroom was in the back left corner of the house, facing the back yard and the fence. Between the fence and the tall trees on the neighbor's side and the bamboo on my family's side, it was a shady spot—my room and, to an extent, the whole house.

When I walked out, the bathroom was on my right and then Katy's room. She had painted her room a bright tangerine and some other festive color, and decoupaged pages from old Archie comics onto her closet door.

One time, years ago now, Alana sent me a recording of late-stage Elvis performing in Vegas because it made her think of me.

Grey but warmer outside. I hear the landlord's car door shut and the timbre of her car's engine. I feel a diffuse energy today. Patsy tells me she wants up and stands on my chest alternately licking my nose and looking out the window. Regretting all the chocolate eggs I popped in my mouth last night. I inherited my susceptibility to sugar from my mother, who also struggles to have just one sweet thing. Listened to Jina give a talk last night on zoom and today I thought about how she found her cat when most other people would have stopped looking. Where there's breath, there's hope, as the saying goes. But when the only breaths perceptible to you are the moist catlike exhalations of spring, bedizening every leaf outside... When we say, "outside," it means outside the house, or House, a structure within which dew doesn't fall—or is it rise? Bethany's call to let what's in my little alembic boil over has been sitting in my inbox for four days. I'm so used to courting intelligibility in the role of a poet (close enough) that when I am hailed as an alchemist, I'm flummoxed. So accustomed have I become to brushing the live wire with the skin on the back of my hand, as one would the hand of a crush— sparking the little hairs, music arcing through the air—that to grasp the thing has become almost anathema. Would I taste bitter lime? Would my bones carbonize? Would I have to sacrifice distance and deferral, to which I have become attached, first out of necessity, as a coping mechanism, then for their intrinsic pleasures? But come now, this isn't a call to die and ascend and become part of some undifferentiated cosmic consciousness but simply to imagine something beyond the Book as the last word; the witch's cradle versus the bow on the birthday present; the lightning rod that draws charges down into the sand, bypassing the house and rendering lightning harmless—a nonevent—versus the queer position in which Melville places readers of "The Lightning-Rod Man"—standing outside the lightning-rod peddler and his skeptical interlocutor, obliged by the circumstance of this configuration to produce, ah, the synthesis!

El Tiempo

Desperate to sit outside and read poetry aloud with friends. My Spanish lesson today was about el tiempo: la niebla, la tormenta, etc, but then writing this poem I open a new lesson and a slew of new (to me) words como la escarcha, que cubre todo en el invierno, el chubasquero, que es necesitado cuando llueve. There is also la ventisca, which I keep trying to make masculine, grammatically (Freud, don't @ me), and finally escampar, as in: Espero que el tiempo escampe en la primavera. Pienso que la niebla es la mas belleza de todas formas de la clima. Eso es por qué escrivé un poema sobre la niebla o, si quieres, en que la niebla es una metáfora de la indeterminación y ambigüedad de la existencia—reforzada con fuentes literarias. Los sospechosos de siempre: Francis Ponge, un poeta fenomenológico, traducido por Karen Volkman, Mei-mei Berssenbrugge, cuyas poemas exudan una energía curativea y Alice Notley, reina de lo negativa, y por eso, adecuada para representar el oscuridad de la niebla. Today it isn't the fog which charms but the wind which torments me, scraping the branches across the windowpane, slipping through the cracks of this old house like a dagger between ribs. What a violent thought! But it was just a f'r'instance—a literary touch, condensing into a phrase like those which O'Brien (in The Third Policeman) and Dostoevsky (Crime and Punishment) expand into an entire novel. What is a novel? I live at the edge of history, a blasted plain, where an accursed wind prevents anyone from stacking pages in sufficient number to constitute a novel.

Midnight Movie

It's raining and my eyes are dilated. I've watched the same dumb show ten times as I've grown further left. I mean that it no longer comforts me, being a vision of a world I don't share. So why am I watching it? I wish I had a tumbler of whiskey and a hand-rolled cigarette, though I no longer smoke. I picture sheltering it with my cupped hand, the back of which is wet with rain, and cold because of it. Some droplets slip through, moistening the cigarette, such that I have to pull harder for a mouthful of smoke and steam. I'm searching for laughter and freedom and care. From the world. The smell of the unstained cedar wood of the shed, the cobwebs of robust Texan spiders and an air-powered stapler. A pneumatic drill press. I don't know what that is. What are all these white cabinets and granite countertops for if not. Poetry and queerness crop up amidst the extremisms of the followers of the Christian lord, highly normalized in Texas. Normalisms crop up in the poetry and queerness of the word, my proper name, a single identifier. But it's not that against which my bile rises up, it's another thing, the missing midnight movie. What was going to have been showing? And candy smuggled in. Teeth and health and rectitude: a USian morality. I never say America anymore unless I mean something bigger than this hateful net cast across dry Denver and the hoof-stamped plains. I fucking hope it rains on Denver tonight unless that is contraindicated for the health of its slacking tubercular wights. Do you see the double-doubleness of my mind? As if I could hex a city and startle myself with my own power, rather than struggling to imagine a billionaire within the gossamer frame of this night music. We're all topping a billionaire from the bottom tonight.

Hymns to the Night

Never doubt the power of the night wowie zowie waking up
into the discovery that night logic is still operative but only for
you and some people don't have anyone there they can rouse
to wakefulness and ask to sit with them. Someone they trust
at the other end of a phoneline, too. Waking up I felt like a
limb had fallen asleep from a pinched off nerve, a lessening of
oxygenated blood, and that limb was my head. Don't romanticize
night logic, although you're tempted to, by dint of a youthful
exposure to Novalis. Was it *Hymns to the Night*? No, it was
someone else and you can't remember her name. The suffering
romantic—that appealed to your adolescent sensibilities—and
the capacity to reenact the errors of Robert Graves and that all
the more thoughtlessly for having come second with respect to
enacting them. But are we that much more responsible for our
performance of the content of the monologues from the theater
of a life lived in time, linear, one-way, birth to death, however
repetitive? Although Husserl, if memory serves, allowed that his
transcendental ego would outlast him. I suppose at the moment
he found that a comfort. I know I have. Have what? Tried to put
women on a pedestal because (or so I thought) I couldn't be one.
This is not a typical trans poem, I just needed that log to toss into
the poem's metaphysical engine, powered by obliquities, powered
by what: one single idea, elaborated with tinsel, basically to the
effect of: don't eat the fairy food, or if you prefer: beware of Greeks
bearing gifts. Then what? For those who have eaten it. The deed
is done, the die is cast. Psychically, I am knocked onto my ass,
body dangling dangerously outside of consensus reality. And yet

enough of me remains, bound with obligations to that reality to answer queries with the customary form. Else I'd be found out and known to be mad, and knowing that, people would think that they knew me, or enough about me to bind me with their knowing.

One, two, three, four

One, two, three… I'm anxious. We're about to move. Britt and I
met with the fertility doctor about IVF. I'm in the thick of reading
The Life of the Mind but when I try to explain its arguments they
fall apart in my hand like wet bread. I invited Una to the reading,
but she didn't come. Ho hum. I figured she wouldn't anyway, but
every time there's a short burst of contact I start to reach out as if
we were in a continuity as opposed to an intermittency. I only read
three poems anyway. I've been waking up into anxiety. Leaden
limbs and the sensation of being a little green plastic army guy
dropped into a drainpipe deeper than my kid arms can reach.
My sister said I should go to the doctor and get some pills for it.
Xanax? Everything is coming down from the shelves and into
boxes. Suddenly, that's all she wrote about the house we lived in
for five years. Okay well that's not totally true, I can explain how
Arendt explains that you don't think about someone when you
are present with them. It's only after, when you are at a remove,
that you can think about them. And if you are thinking about them
while they are present, that means you have withdrawn within
yourself and so are at a kind of metaphysical remove, despite being
physically present. B and I have sex on Sunday. Afterward, I call
them Merlin, because they are a pussy wizard. They keep figuring
out new stuff to do with my body, but they say we are figuring
it out together and I guess we are. (I will probably have to take
the sex stuff out if this gets published.) After that I go running. I
always think I have more time than I do, coming back just before
the reading starts, face pink with exertion. Continuing my utter
musical withdrawal from the present with Sisqó's "Thong Song,"

Blackstreet's "No Diggity," Missy Elliot's "Get Your Freak On." I feel like I can finally occupy and enjoy 90s playful raunchy stuff now. I bookmark a Mattilda Bernstein Sycamore take on nostalgia to read later. What does all this restless activity avail me? One, two, three, four… When you are writing you can shuffle the events around so that they are out of sequence. In the optometrist's office, waiting for my eyes to achieve their full dilation, I meditate, doing the thing someone taught me so many years ago, where I count my breaths to ten. If you lose track, just start over. Maybe it was at the Austin Zen Center, two blocks from the shitty apartment where I lived with my ex and our turtle, smoking cigarettes and drinking Spaten Optimator from the coop across the street.

Pavilion

Sip coffee and hawk loogies while the birds of springtime sound in Kathy's garden. Lynn's new book is out so I text Emily and Amanda. Lynn's poetic magic bound us in friendship. The trick is a reading in a garden, with a bonfire, of long poems like Alice Notley's "At Night the States," or, better yet, poems of your own composition. Spring wraps its garlands around even the plain and unassuming columns of my sentences. Not to be embarrassed about the things that give you genuine pleasure. I've been working a knife in the crack between grace and Christianity. The way I was always a little embarrassed to enjoy Nietzsche, as if he were too adolescent or something. Spring's structures are provisional, as transitory as adolescence in the life cycle of the human organism. Ephemeral: that's the word I was looking for, with its pillowy ph soughing like a pink cloud in Watteau's "Embarkation for Cythera" or a fairy tale princess who becomes separated from her retinue in the Forest, connotative of wildness, and wanders, bereft any familiar sight, until she comes upon a clearing in which a pavilion, gaily decked out, forms a container for the merry making of richly caparisoned lords and ladies, the likes of which she has never seen before. Welcomed as an honored guest into their fête, she departs in satisfied bewilderment. She returns in company, but the pavilion is gone, as are the lords and ladies, as, indeed, is any sign that foot or hoof has ever trod the grass of the clearing.

Ghazal With Ill-Chosen Repeating Word

The loogie that you hawked and spat was pearlescent,
the way that cum, too, can be pretty because pearlescent.

Deep draughts of diesel exhaust medicate my lust for the city,
as fog renders even a missed bus pearlescent.

There's a place where azure firmament gives way to black void.
Anoxia before dying renders life's lack pearlescent.

I can visit you at noon and then take you after to Umass—
I, your mother-of-pearl; you, my daughter, pearlescent.

My latest earworm is Elliott Smith's "Waltz, No. 2"
The nostalgic finds the past's songs, even its faults, pearlescent.

Please don't print this in Zoe Tuck's Collected Poems!
I want the memory of my verses positive, selective; pearlescent.

Notes

Time Travel

› Several of these poems were written for donors to The Trans Asylum Seeker Support Network, or TASSN, which is a border abolitionist direct action and mutual aid collective focused on supporting transgender asylum seekers in crossing the border, getting out of detention, securing housing, legal support, healthcare, transportation, and comprehensive daily financial and material support, building thriving lives and communities, and winning their asylum cases.

Art Criticism

› I watched Matthew Barney's *Cremaster III* twice at the Dobie Theatre—the "bijoux" named in the poem—in Austin, TX when it played there in 2003. Barney spins out a mythos around goo, Celtic mythology, Masonic rites, metempsychosis, and the sexualization of the American automobile.

Coneys in Vilnius

› A self-translation:

I could write a poem in Spanish
(although I never have), but
when I began to write in English,
the poem—which should be about Vilnius—suffered
a short circuit because I fell
in a rabbit hole
about the tragic history of the city in the 20th century.

So, instead of writing a poem about Vilnius in English,
I write you a poem about my failure
in writing about Vilnius in English, in Spanish.
In the gap between the two languages,
where they unspeakable things go.

Samson's Riddle
› Samson's Riddle: "Out of the eater came something to eat, and out of the strong came something sweet."

No Sunlight
› Hannah Arendt's discusses the Vita Activa and the Vita Contemplativa at length in *The Human Condition*
› Jos Charles's talk, *Lyric Relation*, delivered December 3rd, 2020 at the Poetry Project. https://www.poetryproject.org/library/recordings/video-archives/video-lyric-relation-with-jos-charles

My opposites
› *Rilke and Andreas-Salomé: A Love Story in Letters*, translated by Edward Snow and Michael Winkler (W. W. Norton & Company, 2008).

In the bath I didn't take
› December 2011 port shutdown in Oakland

Smol Bean
› Ray Bradbury's *The Halloween Tree* (Alfred A. Knopf, 1972)

Mouthfeel
› Wikipedia "Mutualist usufruct" (https://en.wikipedia.org/wiki/Anarchist_economics)

> This poem pilfers a phrase or two from Emily Dickinson's "Because I could not stop for death."

Chassis
> "The Lost History of Socialism's DIY Computer," Michael Eby, Jacobin. (https://jacobin.com/2020/08/computer-yugoslavia-galaksija-voja-antonic/)

A boring poem
> NSF's Ice Core Facility website (https://icecores.org/)

Janáček's Enigmatic Tones
> For more on the pedagogy of Bethany Ides, including Investigative Operatics, see: https://wavefarm.org/wf/archive/q5v35d.

Dear LL and VS
> "Diary of a Bookseller" by Noah Ross, Open Space
> The quote that begins, "I'm still with you in that…" is from Alice Notley's "At Night the States."

Your valid extended play remix
> For more on the lesbianism of Eleanor Roosevelt, see Eleanor and Hick: The Love Affair That Shaped a First Lady by Susan Quinn.
> For the Belladonna* recording referenced in this poem, and other recordings of Akilah Oliver reading, see her PennSound page: https://writing.upenn.edu/pennsound/x/Oliver.php.

Well-known eccentrics
> The Wikipedia entry on Jennifer Gale has been deleted, but

can be viewed via the Internet Archive's Wayback Machine at https://web.archive.org/web/20111124025909/https://en.wikipedia.org/wiki/Jennifer_Gale.

La la la
› Akilah Oliver, from *the she said dialogues: flesh memory* (Nightboat Books, 2021)

Alternative Poetry
› Daniel Davidson's *Culture* (Krupskaya Books, 2002)

A Poem About Simone Weil
› Is in dialogue with her book *The Need for Roots,* translated by Arthur Wills (Routledge Classics, 2002)

Early Hominids
› This poem is in dialogue with the Radiolab episode, "Neanderthal's Revenge" (https://radiolab.org/episodes/neanderthals-revenge).

Barking
› "Cool Women: When the apparently hard-edged rejection of identity betrays a hidden sentimentalism" by Elena Comay del Junco, published February 21, 2020 in *The New Inquiry* (https://thenewinquiry.com/cool-women/).

500,000 people dead of COVID in the US & I'm sorry that being on my HD tip is how I process it
› This figure is now estimated at 1.07 million as of November 2022.

I'm not as bad as I pretended to be

› Soleida Ríos' *The Dirty Text* (Kenning Editions, 2018).

› This poem references the child migrant detention facility in Carrizo Springs, TX.

› Per Wikipedia, "*Red Shoe Diaries* is an American anthology erotic drama series that aired on Showtime cable network from 1992 to 1997"

The Women's Building

› Epigraph from *The Newly Born Woman*, by Hélène Cixous and Catherine Clément, translated by Betsy Wing (University of Minnesota Press, 1986).

› The Women's Building has been the site of the San Francisco Women's Center since 1978/9. "Becoming Visible: The First Black Lesbian Conference" was held there in in 1980.

Hymns to the Night

› *Robert Graves: The Years with Laura: 1926-1940* (Penguin Books, 1992)

› Edmund Husserl's *The Idea of Phenomenology*, translated by Lee Hardy (Kluwer Academic Publishers, 1999)

One, two, three, four

› "The Future Is Coming, That's a Fact: Mattilda Bernstein Sycamore and Sarah Schulman in Conversation." *The Millions.* 2019 (https://themillions.com/2019/01/the-future-is-coming-thats-a-fact-mattilda-bernstein-sycamore-and-sarah-schulman-in-conversation.html).

Acknowledgments

"Time Travel" was published under the previous title "[7 August 2020]" in the Polymorphous *per* Verse issue of *Arc Poetry Magazine*. "Coneys in Vilnius," "Samson's Riddle," "Anyone else listening in 2020?" and "What's Happening in the Troposphere" were published in *The Canary*, Issue 7. "Poem for Hoa" and "Well-known eccentrics" were published in *G U E S T*, issue 18. "Dragging my feet" and "The Women's Building" were published in Belladonna* Chaplet #266: *May No Emails Find You*. "Midnight Movie" and "No Sunlight" were published in *Northern New England Review*, Volume 42. Grateful acknowledgment to the editors of these publications!

Deep thanks to my partner in love and poetry, Britt Billmeyer-Finn, my family, and the friends who animate the matrix of sociality in which these poems were written. Thanks to Adie and the rest of the Fonograf Editions/BUNNY team. Special thanks to Audra Puchalski for the use of her beautiful art for the cover and to Amy Berkowitz for helping me title both these poems and the book itself. Deep gratitude for the support of J, Bridget, Audra, Avren, Sam, Emme, Geoff, Alice, Carrie, Anna, Ariel, María José, Katy, Taleen, Rebekah, Rachel, Vidhi, Nikita, Eric, Lindsay, Jina, eva, Zefyr, Jess, Victor, Amanda, Kate, Charlie Jane, Shana, Lauren, Elisa, il'ia, Chloe, Frank, Serena, Denise, Faith, MC, Tim, Gion, and Scout.

About the Author

Zoe Tuck was born in Texas, became a person in California, and now lives in Massachusetts. She is the author of *Terror Matrix* (Timeless, Infinite Light) and the chapbooks "Vape Cloud of Unknowing" (Belladonna*) and the "The Book of Bella" (DoubleCross Press), the latter of which is bound in a dos-a-dos edition with Emily Hunerwadel's "Peach Woman". In addition to teaching private creative writing and literature classes, Zoe is the co-host of The But Also reading series with Britt Billmeyer-Finn and the co-editor of Hot Pink Magazine with Emily Bark Brown. Since 2019, she has been an active member of the Belladonna* Collaborative, where she has co-curated both the Close Distances and the In-Flux reading series.

FONO
GRA꒕

1. **Eileen Myles**—*Aloha/irish trees* (LP)

2. **Rae Armantrout**—*Conflation* (LP)

3. **Alice Notley**—*Live in Seattle* (LP)

4. **Harmony Holiday**—*The Black Saint and the Sinnerman* (LP)

5. **Susan Howe & Nathaniel Mackey**—*STRAY: A Graphic Tone* (LP)

6. **Annelyse Gelman & Jason Grier**—*About Repulsion* (EP)

7. **Joshua Beckman**—*Some Mechanical Poems To Be Read Aloud* (print)

8. **Dao Strom**—*Instrument/ Traveler's Ode* (print; cassette tape)

9. **Douglas Kearney & Val Jeanty**—*Fodder* (LP)

10. **Mark Leidner**—*Returning the Sword to the Stone* (print)

11. **Charles Valle**—*Proof of Stake: An Elegy* (print)

12. **Emily Kendal Frey**—*LOVABILITY* (print)

13. **Brian Laidlaw and the Family Trade**—*THIS ASTER: adaptations of Emile Nelligan* (LP)

14. **Nathaniel Mackey and The Creaking Breeze Ensemble**—*Fugitive Equation* (compact disc)

15. *FE Magazine* (print)

16. **Brandi Katherine Herrera**—*MOTHER IS A BODY* (print)

17. **Jan Verberkmoes**—*Firewatch* (print)

18. **Krystal Languell**—*Systems Thinking with Flowers* (print)

19. **Matvei Yankelevich**—*Dead Winter* (print)

20. **Cody-Rose Clevidence**—*Dearth & God's Green Mirth* (print)

21. **Hilary Plum**—*Hole Studies* (print)

22. **John Ashbery**—*Live at Sanders Theatre, 1976* (LP)

23. **Alice Notley**—*The Speak Angel Series* (print)

24. **Alice Notley**—*Early Works* (print)

25. **Joshua Marie Wilkinson**—*Trouble Finds You* (print)

26. **Timmy Straw**—*The Thomas Salto* (print)

27. **Audre Lorde**—*At Fassett Studio, 1970* (LP)

28. **Gabriel Palacios**—*A Ten Peso Burial For Which Truth I Sign* (print)

29. **Isabel Zapata, trans. Robin Myers**—*A Whale Is a Country* (print)

30. **Callum Angus**—*Cataract* (print)

31. **Eds. Dao Strom & Jyothi Natarajan**—*A Mouth Holds Many Things: A De-Canon Hybrid-Literary Collection* (print)

32. **Cody-Rose Clevidence**—*The Grimace of Eden, Now* (print)

33. **Jaydra Johnson**—*Low: Notes on Art and Trash* (print)

34. **Jaime Gil de Biedma**—*If Only For a Moment (I'll Never Be Young Again)* (print)

35. **Esther Kondo Heller**—*AR:RANGE:MENTS* (print)

36. **Ahmad Almallah**—*Wrong Winds* (print)

37. **Kimberly Alidio**—*Traceable Relation* (print)

38. **Sara Gilmore**—*The Green Lives* (print)

39. **Darcie Dennigan**—*Little Neck* (print)

40. **Nora Claire Miller**—*Groceries* (print)

41. **Rachel Rahmé**—*Mercurial, or is that Liberty?* (print)

42. **Eileen Myles**—*Bird Watching and Their First Three Books of Poetry* (print)

43. **Kristen Gleason**—*The Wallet and Other Thefts* (print)

44. **Xuela Zhang**—*To Compare* (print)

Fonograf Editions is a registered 501(c)(3) nonprofit organization. Find more information about the press at: fonografeditions.com.

1. **Warren Longmire**—*BIRD/DIZ [an erased history of bebop]* (print)

2. **Bill Carty**—*We Sailed on the Lake* (print)

3. **Zoe Tuck**—*Bedroom Vowel* (print)

4. **Michael Wheaton**—*Home Movies* (print)

5. **Jennifer Quartararo**—*An Aribtrary Formation of Unspecified Value* (print)

6. **Matt Broaddus**—*Deeper the Tropics* (print)

7. **Katie Naughton**—*Debt Ritual* (print)

8. **Marina Blitshteyn**—*Landguage/Mirror Me* (print)

Inspired by the work of the multitudinous artist Ray Johnson, BUNNY is an imprint of Fonograf Editions. Publishing a wide variety of works, BUNNY is looking towards the future while thinking about the past.

2 04

9 781737 803690